AF269751

EVER *the* BEGINNING

EVER *the* BEGINNING

ALLEN T. BROWN

with JEEYOON KIM

GREENLEAF
BOOK GROUP PRESS

Published by Greenleaf Book Group Press
Austin, Texas
www.gbgpress.com

Distributed by Greenleaf Book Group

For ordering information or special discounts for bulk purchases, please contact Greenleaf Book Group at PO Box 91869, Austin, TX 78709, 512.891.6100.

Design and composition by Greenleaf Book Group and Jonathan Lewis
Cover design by Greenleaf Book Group and Jonathan Lewis

Publisher's Cataloging-in-Publication data is available.

Print ISBN: 979-8-88645-360-7

eBook ISBN: 979-8-88645-361-4

To offset the number of trees consumed in the printing of our books, Greenleaf donates a portion of the proceeds from each printing to the Arbor Day Foundation. Greenleaf Book Group has replaced over 50,000 trees since 2007.

Printed in the United States of America on acid-free paper

25 26 27 28 29 30 31 32   10 9 8 7 6 5 4 3 2 1

First Edition

To Patricia—the love of my life

Contents

Preface

When do people make the first memory of their life?

I'm standing in my crib, mesmerized by the texture of the wallpaper. Bright sunlight is pouring into the room through the window. Outside, the grasses of a fully grown green meadow are dancing with the wind. Across the room, next to the open door, I see my newborn baby brother James lying asleep in his crib. I am observing the space, feeling the heat of the room.

Maybe I was thinking about something specific or maybe not making sense of anything at all, but I remember this scene vividly, like a movie, as the first memory of noticing myself, Allen Brown—and the world outside of me.

I must have been about 14 months old in this first memory of taking in the meadow, the sunlight, and the room that belonged to me and my baby brother. I am 91 now. Life has been passing through me and has shaped me with events and memories. I remember some events, and there are others that I don't remember anymore. If you ask me today what the best moment of my life has been, I will say, "this moment, right now," without hesitation. I am living the dream. I am fully alive, enjoying everything life can offer me. I am content in more profound ways than I ever could have been in my youth.

IIIIIIIIIIIIIIIIIIIIIIIIIIIIIIIIIIIIIIIIIIIII

I'm SITTING TODAY IN a local coffee shop under the pleasant California sun with my morning coffee and a blueberry muffin. I'm daydreaming about my childhood when I was a boy on my father's farm.

I was born in a small town in Michigan, where there were only about ten houses. There was no running water in our house, which was typical back then in the 1930s. We grew our food in the backyard. There were no grocery stores, fancy store-bought cookies, toys, or TV, but my brothers and I played all day in the meadow. The contrast between then and now is too great for me to grasp, and I often shake my head at what has happened to me to allow me to live the life I am living now.

All the people I knew back then chose to live the farm lifestyle for the rest of their lives. I am not downgrading their choices, but I often wonder what separated me from them. I had a dream beyond the farm, and they did not. Do people make certain life choices simply because they are comfortable or convenient? Not because it is what they want? Did they give up even before trying?

IIIIIIIIIIIIIIIIIIIIIIIIIIIIIIIIIIIIIIIIIIIII

On MY FATHER's FARM one day, I remember looking down at some corn seedlings with my two brothers. They were small and barely starting to peek from the earth into the air. I knew these seedlings would turn into at least fifty to seventy ears of corn. I knew I needed nothing to make that magical growth happen except to water them and protect them from harm. That was the first time I understood there were some energy forces out there that I did not understand—the first time I started to be aware of the unseen powers of life.

Someone once said that everyone has a book or two in them. I believe that is true, and so I finally decided to embark on writing my story. I have always been on a quest to find out who I am and how I became who I am now. I have achieved much wisdom, knowledge, friendship, and wealth—things I could never have imagined in my youth. And while you may not know me, my stories are a gift for you from someone who has lived long enough to be able to look back with a broad perspective. I hope my stories are like sitting down together with me in a café, sharing the key, insightful moments of my life over a morning coffee. I hope and intend them to be light, bite-size pieces of the bliss of life.

Finally, deep down, and maybe on a more selfish level, I know my story is ultimately a gift to myself, a way to understand my life better. Perhaps I'll be able to discover a critical pathway. Or, conversely, perhaps I will never find why or how I became who I am, which could be okay too. I believe that much of our lives is guided by our unconscious mind with a force of energy we do not see. I have always been interested in unlocking that unconscious mind to open myself to more extensive perspectives.

My only wish is that you will start to dream about the impossible being possible and that this book helps you to gain the strength and faith to take the first step into the unknown—the potential discovery of yourself.

If the farm boy in the middle of nowhere could dream and make the dream into a reality, you can certainly do it too.

CHAPTER 1

Photography— Learning to See

I have been patiently waiting for the image to appear on a sheet of paper in a darkroom that I set up in my bathroom. I put a roll of film into a mix of chemicals, watching to see how the negative turns into an image. I cross my fingers hoping that the picture that appears reflects what it needs to express. I've never gotten tired of studying images in a darkroom or the creative process in black-and-white film photography. I often spent hours out in nature with a camera, looking for something to call me to be captured.

I was about five years old when my dad gave me a camera with a kit that I could use to develop the negatives. The first photo I ever took was of my father smiling at me in his humble farming clothes. I didn't know what I was doing, yet I was captivated by my father's transformation from the world onto the image on white paper and the concept of seeing through a camera lens. I have kept this image of my father with me since that day; it's been a long time. For me, that day represented curiosity and my desire to learn to see.

I used that simple 35mm film camera throughout my 20s while I traveled through Europe in the military. The process of taking pictures caused me to stop and relish the moments of life I was experiencing. Film cameras differ from modern digital cameras. With digital cameras, you have hundreds and thousands of opportunities to capture a given scene, and you never have to worry about wasting money on canisters of film that may either not capture your scene as you saw it or may even come out blank. Every attempt counts in film cameras. You need to study the location, the object, and the feel of the environment before you click the shutter. I love the beauty of intentionality and the scarcity of film photography.

My desire to learn to see better through the camera grew as I passed through my 20s. I always believed that taking time to learn how to take better photos would ultimately mean I would know how to see the world better. So I took a photography course at Long Beach State College, where I learned how to properly develop negatives. From that point on, I kept knocking on the doors of master photographers such as John Sexton and Morley Baer, attending their professional photographer workshops and taking private lessons.

One afternoon, I joined a group of fellow photographers on a field trip to take photos of nature. We captured beautiful sights with our cameras and then tested with a Polaroid camera to double-check that what we had clicked our shutters on was an accurate image of what we saw. There was no instant playback in film photography, so a Polaroid was the only way to check a photo's composition. Morley Baer, the photographer, happened to pass by. Glancing at my Polaroid, he asked, "What is the subject?" I was just as confused as he was. *What do you mean?* I thought. I stepped back and looked again at my scene. He was right. There was no subject in my photo, but at the same time, there were too many statements. I was trying to say too much, so I ended up with conflicting messages and therefore was saying nothing. I learned that day that there is only one topic. Whether it is a cat, a feather, a mountain valley, or a piece of wood, it doesn't matter. The important thing to remember is that a good photograph expresses only one subject and one feeling.

I have learned that you must take your time when you're photographing an object. Talk to it, question it, walk around it, wait for it—and then wait to listen to it. If you are patient enough, that thing you want to capture will eventually (and always) talk to you. I always thought that I was the one who took the photo, but that couldn't be further from the truth. I was just the mere communicator between the object and the world—channeling and opening the door for it—so it could speak for itself. You have to take time to become friends with whatever it is in front of your camera. What is the tree seeing? What is the tree saying? Once you've made your connection, then click the shutter or press the button. After, look at your photo. Is your image reflecting what the tree told you it wanted to say?

Black-and-white film photography has another layer in the process: a darkroom. Once you capture what you thought you caught, you go into a darkroom, create your chemicals, and adjust them in a way that effectively expresses your preferences. There are millions of ways of expressing tonality between shades of black and white. These subtleties make all the difference. Nothing is better than black-and-white film photography. It's how photographers truly express the feeling of the object they feel. No fancy color images could ever match its unique expression. To me, it is an art. It is poetry.

Throughout this book, you will see black-and-white film photos that I took. I have spent days and months capturing some of these images. I would go to the same spot in the morning and afternoon, and then in the light of sunset, repeating this process until finally, I felt I did some justice to the thing (or scene) I wanted to communicate. I hope you take your time to look at each photograph. Maybe not days, but stop and talk to the photo. That way, you will be more receptive to what you see.

IIIIIIIIIIIIIIIIIIIIIIIIIIIIIIIIIIIIIIII

LEARNING TO SEE IS what I learned through photography. I hope that you start that journey too. For me, it broadens my horizons and the dimensions of my life. It is more than okay to take this journey with your cell phone in your hand. Go for a walk, and then take time until something speaks to you. Think of it as a film camera. Reflect as though you only have a few chances to get the shot before you push the capture button. Learn to slow it down. Learn to communicate. I promise you that this beautiful process of photography will help you to see the world better and to be a more empathetic person in it.

CHAPTER 2

Freedom, Exploration, and My Father

I look back on my childhood with fond memories, and I love the fact that during those days, I had no other pressures in life other than to follow my curiosity where it led me. Sometimes I walked through the nearby woods for miles all day. Everything about nature elicited my interest—from an abstractly shaped rock formation or a line of hundreds of ants carrying food underground to a piece of Native American art on the ground. There were fun tree trunks to jump up and down on, and I was amazed by how the shapes of different giant trees could express emotions to me. I didn't own a watch. But I always knew by the sun's location if it was time to head home for dinner before my parents came looking for me. As long as I was home by dark, no questions were ever asked about my whereabouts. I do vividly remember several occasions when I got lost in the woods, and everywhere I turned, I was surrounded by ominous trees and swamps. I panicked initially on one occasion, without knowing where to go, but then it came to me somehow that I needed to walk in a straight line. People tend to walk in a big circle when they're lost in the woods, so I marked one tree to the next, walking straight. Finally, I led myself out.

I knew it was my responsibility to take care of myself and protect myself. It was a whole different culture back then. From the moment I could walk alone, I was raised "free range." No one was worried about me. I could do anything I wanted. There was a life to explore. I was given the freedom to nurture my endless curiosity.

On the other hand, school was not interesting to me. There were only several kids in the neighborhood in a class for the whole school. I was interested in reading, and I was interested in painting in art class, but I had a hard time seeing any real relation between the life I was living on a farm and the subjects the school was teaching. Nature and the farm were my teachers. Until my university years, my schooling was in the shadow of my history.

My father was a hero in my childhood world. He was able to pick up blocks of concrete from the ground that my brothers and I together couldn't even move an inch. He knew solutions to all the everyday farm troubles and fixed them with ease. In addition to his farm work, he also had another job delivering milk and cream with a horse carriage to houses in nearby towns. He always took one of us boys on his deliveries, which made us feel like we were doing an important job. It also made us proud to be a part of the real world. When he delivered milk to each house, my job was to carry a bottle of cream. I was there to help but felt I mostly went unnoticed by people in general.

However, on one occasion, I was with my father when he went inside the factory to talk with the general manager. I was waiting outside. A moment later, the manager walked outside, knelt down, and talked to me eye to eye. I don't recall what he talked about, but I remember the strong sensation in me that he noticed me and made an effort to talk to me. That unknown man made me feel like I was someone important.

To this day, because of that experience, I make a conscious effort to talk to a little kid with their parents if I see them on the street or in a café. You never know how a real and genuine interaction with a stranger might bring light to their life in a way we can never imagine.

||||||||||||||||||||||||||||||||||||||||||

THE HOUSE WHERE I grew up sat on a dirt road near the railroad tracks about three miles out from Saginaw, Michigan. I lived there with my father, mother, and two brothers. The only other structures around were ten or so houses and a single gas station. Paved streets had not yet arrived, and the only way into this settlement was on a dirt road that was studded with flat tree trunk pieces that had been placed on the dirt roadway to keep the cars from sinking and getting stuck in the mud.

Our house was built for a farm family. There was no refrigerator, no air conditioner, no heater. There was no running water. Yet that house didn't limit us in any way. Mom cooked every meal from scratch with the produce from our farm or from the countryside. I remember going on a long walk to pick wild berries with my brothers. When I returned with a basket full of berries, Mom baked a pie and then made the rest into jam. When we had more than enough vegetables or fruits from the harvest, we preserved them as jams or pickles in Mason jars and stored them in our basement, which was full of homemade dried and canned foods that kept us well-fed during the winter.

Working on the farm was a part of life as a family member. One of the earliest memories of my youth includes feeding chickens and pigs, pulling weeds, milking cows, and planting seeds by hand. As young as eleven years old, I even started to drive a tractor to help my father. All my clothes were secondhand and had many patches. I made my very first purchase with money I earned from working at our farm when I was twelve years old. I walked to a nearby town where I spent twelve dollars on a brand-new pair of pants. I walked home with a huge grin, feeling like a million dollars.

I used to like passing time sitting by the railroad tracks with my two brothers, George and James. We would put stones on the rails and then watch with delight as the train passed by. Anything on the ground became an instant toy or the focus for a game. We would pick up sticks and throw them hard into the vast meadow that stretched out in front of us. "Throw it farther than mine, Allen!" George would challenge me. And with that one stick off the ground, we invented unlimited games that could last for hours. George and James were my best friends growing up. Even when tensions built up between us, my position as the middle child made me good at mediating and knowing how to play just the right card to clear the hot air and make them laugh.

|||||||||||||||||||||||||||||||||||||||||||||

PEOPLE OFTEN CALLED ME a white-haired boy, meaning someone pure. I could do nothing wrong, it seemed. My brothers often got in trouble with my parents, but I didn't. I was undoubtedly getting into the same naughty, boyish mischief as they were, but the only difference was that I knew how to avoid getting caught. In fact, I had learned those very techniques from my brothers and instinctively understood the limits of when to stop.

One evening, I remember my brothers and my parents having a discussion about why our parents spanked us. They told us if we did anything we knew we were not supposed to do, we would get spanked. But if we didn't know what was out of bounds and they knew that too, we would be fine. It was a simple enough rule for me to understand. One day, I was driving the tractor on the dirt road up a steep hill on our farm. I made a bad turn and lost control. The last thing I remembered was the tractor turned on its side, planted flat on the ground. My heart was pumping hard, and I was worried I would be in big trouble with my father. *I might even get spanked*, I thought, as I told him what had happened. But he said nothing, walked to the tractor, and somehow saved the tractor from the ditch. I was still worried and pleasantly surprised when he didn't scold me during dinner. Days later, I asked him why I was not in trouble with the tractor accident. He said, "You didn't know what to do in that situation. All you were trying to do was to help the farm."

I learned a valuable life lesson at that moment: Good intentions are much more important than whatever outcome might result in a situation. Always have a good heart in doing things in life in the first place.

When I look back on my childhood, one sentence I never heard from my parents was, "Be careful." Not that they didn't care about my well-being. Nor was I unaware of the world's dangers. But they allowed me to be free to explore the world without tight boundaries from them. I learned about my surroundings independently, and making a right or wrong choice solely depended on me. Interestingly, I see many parents today having difficulty letting go of their control of their kids. But because of too much protection from their parents, children can often miss out on the learning that comes by making mistakes. These children delay their life lessons from a young age and then risk living inside the cocoon of a safety net as an adult. Without going through the hardship of the caterpillar stage independently, they may never learn to fly as a butterfly. I do not know how much my parents were aware of this mindset consciously, but I am forever grateful for their trust in me and letting me learn the world on my own without planting a seed of unnecessary fear by saying, "Be careful."

You exist here and now. That is more than enough.

|||||||||||||||||||||||||||||||||||||||||||||

CHAPTER 3

Adventures as a Merchant Marine

My family went to church every Sunday, although I don't recall my family being overly religious. Going to church was our family's routine, dressing up with the cleanest clothes we owned. When I was old enough to walk to the church by myself, I was given a job at Sunday school teaching a group of six- and seven-year-old kids.

I had read the Bible from cover to cover twice, but I can't remember exactly how I got roped into the job. Nonetheless, I remember I took the role seriously. Growing up, I was taught not to lie to others or myself and to pursue the truth continuously. They say if you want to master something, try to teach it. Since teaching those foundational principles to young kids, seeking the truth has been embedded in my soul. Do I believe in God? Yes, I do. I learned to let my curiosity take the lead, and, for the rest, God would take care of it.

As soon as I graduated from high school, I procured a job working in a factory that made RV trailers. Immediately, I switched to the night shift since I preferred not going to work when the masses were going. I always liked to choose a path where I could create my own rules.

I often visited a city near our town, Port Huron, in Michigan, where I saw a vast freighter moving under the bridge connecting Michigan to Canada. The gigantic ship moved ever so slowly, as if time had stopped. Then, before I realized it, it disappeared into the distance. I often thought out loud, "I wonder what it would be like to work on one of those freighters?" The ship represented wonder, adventure, and mystery to the farm boy I was.

One hot summer day, a new next-door neighbor moved in. It was quite an event in town. Who are they? Where are they from? My family walked down the path and introduced ourselves. After a little chat, we learned that the man was a skipper on one of those freighters. I perked up with curiosity, thinking, *Can I work there too?* Before I knew it, a formal document was delivered to my house. Officially, I was hired to be a merchant marine!

The following spring, when I was seventeen years old, my brother drove me to the shipyard, where I saw an old steam freighter that had seen action in the Vietnam War. It was hauling iron ore from Canada to Chicago and Ohio. I climbed up aboard the freighter and looked below me, where I saw only two small ladder legs still connecting me to the earth. I gripped the ladder firmly and stepped into the ship with determination.

Seventeen years of history was gone in an instant. I disconnected from my past and slipped into an unknown future. I was once a farm boy; now, I was a merchant marine! I felt a huge sensation of freedom. There was nothing to worry about. I was like a leaf swept along by wind and wave. I didn't look back again. The tingling feeling in my heart told me my adventure was about to begin, but I was not alone. The angels were watching over me.

|||||||||||||||||||||||||||||||||||||||||||

I WAS ON THE ship from March to December, traveling from the Great Lakes to Sault Ste. Marie in Canada, back to Detroit, and then back to Canada. Everything was new and exciting to me at first, but life on the ship was actually pretty rough. People were continuously throwing up from seasickness off the side of the boat. I was confined in rooms with small windows and never an open breeze from the outside. I didn't get to communicate with people from any other part of the boat, just the same four or five people every day. But I soon realized that I was getting paid not for the job I was doing on the freighter but for the life I was getting to live on that boat.

My first position on the freighter was as a coal passer. I shoveled coals and passed them over to the fireman at the boiler. There were eight huge doors where the coal was sent to turn into the steam for the engine. It was the type of physical work that I was used to doing at the farm, except that this environment was dark and hot. I was happy that I was soon promoted to a fireman, then to an oiler. The higher the promotion meant more responsibility. The oiler's job was to check the temperature of all crankshaft bearings as the engine cycled, so every twenty minutes, I checked the bearings by touching them with my finger. I needed to be awake and careful with this part of the freighter because the boiler could explode at any moment if it were not balanced and rechecked continuously.

One night, I was performing my usual checking routine alone. When I looked up and saw the gauge, my heart jumped. There was no water in the meter. I ran as fast as I could to the engineer, who, once I told him, could barely get any words out, he was in such shock. But I understood that if the boiler got any hotter, we'd all die instantly. His face was white as a ghost and his words were garbled. I grabbed his arm and screamed, "COME ON!!!" We ran and opened the water valves one by one to allow water into the boiler as fast as we could. We looked at each other in a soaking sweat, in despair. We did everything we could do, but nothing changed. *Maybe this is how all ends . . .* That was the moment we heard *Boom!* and the sound of the water roaring into the boiler. We were still shaking, in shock, watching our lives emerge from death. The four pistons moved up and down, unconcerned. Life continued as if nothing had happened, and the quiet night with the peaceful sound of water in the background confirmed that all was well.

Now, I ask what might have been our fate if I had not been promoted to be an oiler for that fearful night. Growing up on a farm, I had one rule in my system: If the tractor was stuck, "unstuck" it! There was no second choice, no second chance. Just do it. Whatever it was that needed doing, there was no time to ponder. There was only time to simply *do.*

That mentality of *just do it* has served me well over the years. Whenever I faced a challenge, I responded intuitively and quickly. Often in life, you don't have the luxury of time to think. You have to follow your instinct and make it happen. Time is precious. On the night of the boilers, quick thinking possibly saved many lives, including mine.

Don't waste your time. Sometimes, life doesn't wait for you.

Balance of life and beauty. Nature is our best teacher.

CHAPTER 4

European Military Life

The year was 1955. I was 21 years old. The war in Vietnam was in full swing. My older brother, George, had already been sent years earlier. I received the official notice that Uncle Sam had found me too. I was to join the Army. There weren't any choices. One day, they told me I'd get picked up by the bus on its way down to Detroit. I didn't question why I had to be there, and once again, physical basic training was easy for me. Marching, carrying heavy backpacks, and using guns came naturally to the farm boy.

Then I was on the train to New York and after that on a ship for seven days straight.

There was a rumor that we might go to Germany, but no one shared clear directions or plans with soldiers. All I can say is that everyone looked upset and unsettled. No one had any idea about their futures. I had no idea where we were headed, but Germany sounded familiar. I had grown up with the German community in my neighborhood. There had even been German prisoners of war marching by my house, and, being young, I waved to them excitedly. They happily waved back to me. I knew they were good people regardless of the war.

Many soldiers suffered from seasickness, so there was lots of throwing up over the side of the boat. Since I was used to being on a ship as a merchant marine, the rocky ship felt like home to me. Separate orders were given to each unit: Clean the boat, work in the kitchen, or help to organize the weapons. I figured out quickly that no one knew what was really happening, including who was present on the ship. That was when I found myself a little brig in the ship's basement and decided to hide there (while everyone else was working). I only came out for food. As expected, no one noticed that I wasn't working. My nature was to always try to find an opposite way of doing things from what everyone else was doing. Even an army didn't stop me from finding my path of looking for a better way!

We eventually arrived in Germany and boarded a train for the city of Bad Kreuznach. Outside the window, I could see gorgeous architecture, churches, beautiful countryside, hills, and mountains. The new foreign view expanded my mind and my thinking almost instantly. I was in a new world. Something unknown, something exciting. I felt a different person within me was awakening.

I thought learning German might be a smart thing to do, so I picked up a book of German vocabulary on the train. I read it and kept studying. I don't know where this hunger for learning came from, but eventually, I taught myself enough of the language to have basic communication capability. The farm boy—who had had no interest in books—suddenly discovered that there was a value in knowledge. That was my first encounter with the power of learning.

My fellow soldiers must have witnessed my hunger to learn. They took me under their wings and off to city libraries, where they showed me books on Shakespeare, Mozart, history, and philosophy. I was in awe of the volume of books and their solemn presence in the space. The libraries were always located in the centers of each city, and we walked through the downtowns and listened to live classical concerts. The soldiers were from many different states in America, and they shared their life stories with me. Almost every day, I would find a note from one of them on my bunk correcting how I spoke English! There wasn't anything harsh about their instruction, just a matter-of-fact approach with love and care. They willingly each took their roles to teach me to speak a better version of English, and they encouraged me to believe that one day, I would attend a university.

Forever will I be indebted to those boys. They enabled me to see a bigger world. They planted the seed of desire to learn and go to college that had never occurred to me before. Suddenly, I had dreams and goals in my mind: One day, I would go to the University of Michigan.

Once on the base, I heard about an opportunity to join the European ski patrol. Immediately, I thought that sounded more interesting than playing soldier. And wearing ski gear looked cooler than a US Army uniform. I told the officer that I would write down a recommendation for a possible ski patrol recruit. They didn't ask me if I could ski, so I said nothing. They just assumed. Of course, I had never skied before, but it didn't matter. I went down to the Alps and took a week of ski lessons. I read books about ski techniques and absorbed the language of a skier until I could talk like an experienced one. Later, I returned to the Alps and took the ski patrol test. I passed with flying colors and became a ski patrol member.

On a sunny, snowy mountain, one of the ski patrol instructors complimented my skiing. I thanked him, but something within said to me, *Who the hell is he to judge me? Only I judge me. That is my responsibility and mine alone.* I was amazed at the thought. It was my thought, but it came from somewhere else. This was a new person. Who *is* this guy called Allen?

A winter season as a ski patrol was a dream job. We got paid by the US government for skiing in the Alps of Italy, Austria, and Germany. Our job as ski patrol was to search for lost skiers. We always found them. But it was also very easy for us to take a wrong turn and end up somewhere we weren't supposed to be.

The winter was about to be over, which meant the ski season would come to an end. Our fellow ski patrols discussed returning to our primary bases. Mine was Bad Kreuznach. A close friend, Jim Speier, and I discussed the possibility that Bad Kreuznach had long since forgotten about us. We decided it was time for a vacation. Jim "borrowed" some seven-day leave of absence papers and signed them as a captain Phillip J. Lawless. We headed for Rome and Pompei, then Barcelona and Monaco. We even walked into the casino and made easy money. We cruised through a shabby but fantastic lifestyle. We got fifty-cent bottles of wine and slept on beaches. We only ate one meal a day in a restaurant. Two buddies joined us at some point. As exciting as our detour vacation was, it was eventually time to go back.

Sometimes you need to step way back to have a better perspective on the entire landscape.

CHAPTER 5

The University of Michigan

During my military service, with fellow soldiers nudging me, I acknowledged that a college education was a necessary next step for me. Up to that point, I had never considered college. Not even once during high school did I desire a higher education or think it was even a possibility. However, after my experience of seeing the globe through a war, I became aware that there were broader horizons and a bigger world for me to study, absorb, and learn from.

I remember the day I arrived in Ann Arbor to test to see if I could be accepted to the University of Michigan. It was an all-day test on various topics. From my perspective growing up in a small town in Michigan, the University of Michigan was known for its excellence and difficulty getting in. I'd never thought I could apply to this very reputable university. After all, I felt all along that academia was not my forte. As I continued, the tests were a struggle, and I knew I was not doing a good job. An education from a small town didn't prepare me for anything like them. With each of the numerous tests, I sensed that the university was more and more out of my reach.

By the end of the day, I was exhausted. A counselor stepped into my room and asked if I could manage a couple of additional tests before I was finished. I let out a big sigh but said yes. Luckily, the next two tests were about common sense, and I had the feeling that I nailed those. After all, my childhood had taught me all about common sense—from farming to working on a freighter and having military experience. Everything I had done required being awake and engaging in constant problem-solving—which I had no choice but to learn.

While waiting for my test results, I did some mountain climbing and read books every day. One thing I always loved was reading. My curiosity made me comfortable within the world of books.

Finally, I received a response. A letter had arrived.

I couldn't believe it! I had made it into a university that I had never even dreamed of. During my meeting with a university professor to discuss my major, he said most students went to university in order to make more money or get a job with a big paycheck. Still, I remember he commented that a university should also be a place where you learn how to think.

"What do you see as any weakness in your education up to now?" he asked, and I said, "literature." He added that if a person can improve their way of thinking, they can do anything. So, following his advice, I chose my weakness as a major: English literature and philosophy. And that was how my adventure in understanding began.

University life was every bit as challenging to me as I had expected. I was continually exposed to—sometimes even overwhelmed by—knowledge that I couldn't have fathomed before. The philosophy classes were past challenging. One professor would write concepts on the blackboard with both hands at the same time. When the end-of-class bell rang, he just walked out, saying nothing. I was forced to take responsibility to step up and grow up. Although I often felt it was all too much for my mind to grasp, and I remember studying from morning to night the final year, it was challenging, and I didn't want the opportunity to pass by me without realizing true growth.

During my time at Michigan, I was required to do a lot of writing on philosophy and literature. It was not a simple or an easy task. I remember one assignment about defining God being particularly challenging. I didn't know how to explain something that did not openly reveal who or what he was. I knew my thinking had to become more flexible and more plastic. One of my friends, Dick Light, helped me a lot with my assignments, underlining areas that needed more work or editing. As a result, I would rewrite and rewrite many times over. I sensed that real change was happening during that editing process while I was dealing with an abstract concept. I noticed an improvement in my writing and realized it was making my thinking more transparent. I was transforming, stepping outside of my own cocoon. And I was beginning to see beyond the everyday world.

Before I could graduate, I was required to present a paper before a class. At that point, I saw a different Allen. I saw someone who was unafraid, standing in front of his peers, elaborating his points confidently. I knew how far I had come. With great coaching and much falling down and getting up again, I left Ann Arbor a different person from the one who had arrived there.

My mother's hands. She raised three boys on a farm, yet
I never once heard a negative word or a complaint from
her. These were hands that were eternally helping others

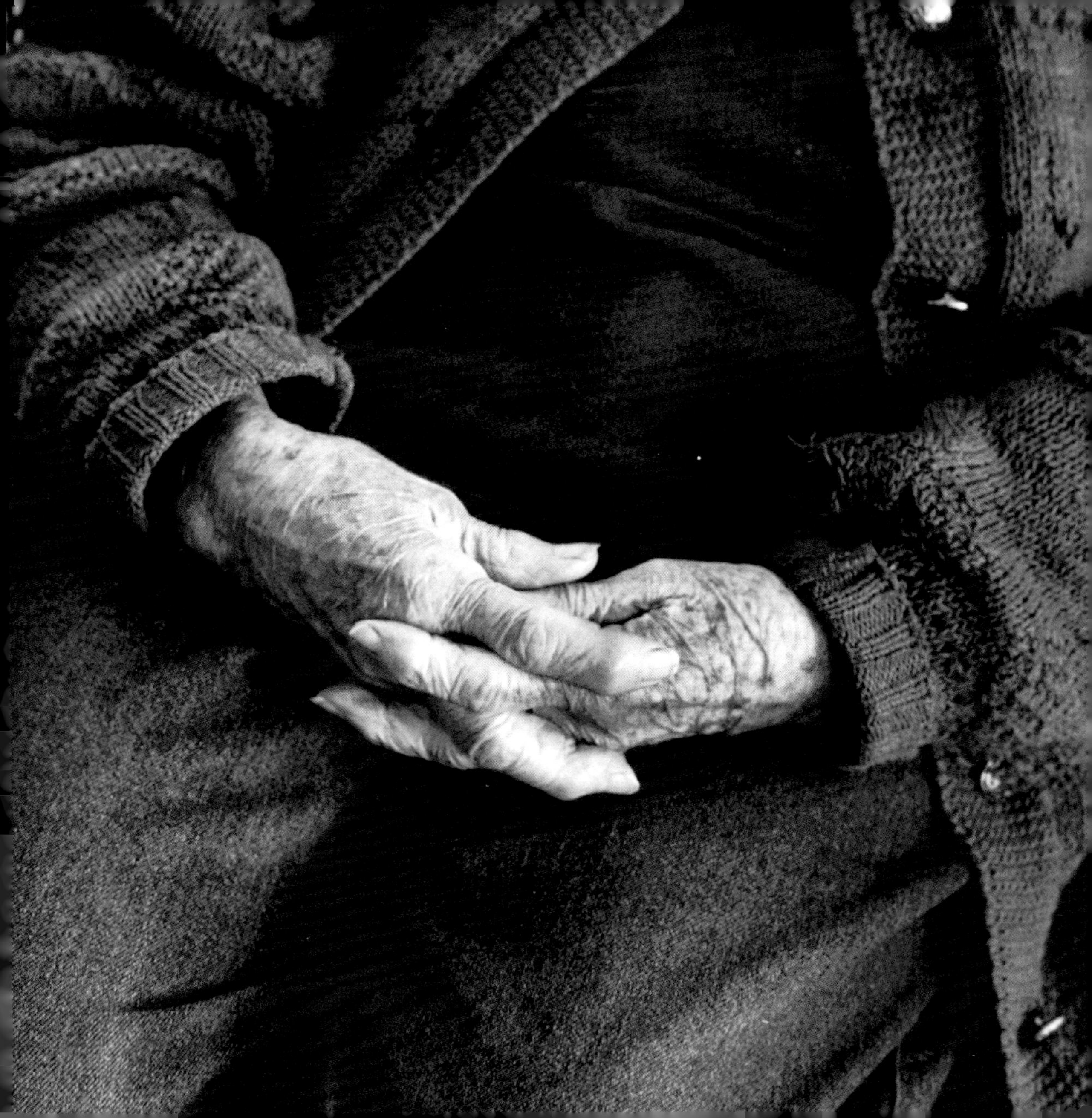

A Land of Possibility

After working for an artificial cattle inseminator for several weeks after graduating from the University of Michigan, I was ready to leave the farmland. I arrived in Colorado with whatever of my belongings could fit in the trunk of my car, hoping to find work. My first job there was managing a six-unit apartment building in Denver. I had no prior knowledge about managing apartments, but I learned quickly—everything from how to unclog a shower drain to how to paint walls. The biggest bonus of that job was that I lived rent free. I worked hard, and I worked long hours, taking any other possible small jobs that came my way. There was not one moment in which I was idle.

One of the tenants in the apartment building worked as a city surveyor. He liked my desire to work hard and immediately hired me to work with him on a job in Vail.

We drove through mountains from Denver and got to work surveying the city's water system for future homes and buildings. We pounded stakes, measured, and recorded the boundary of the town. Back then, there was only one house with hot water in that mountain town. I am not sure if I should even call Vail a town, because in those days, there wasn't even a grocery store. It was basically a nonexistent town, given that we were there to establish its boundaries.

Peter Seibert came up with the idea of developing a ski town in this bare landscape. I could only see acres of empty land, some cabins for sheepherders, and the difficulty of making a road through the mountains. But Peter saw the potential of building the best ski resort in America at some point in the future by inviting wealthy people to invest millions of dollars. I once had the honor of skiing and conversing with Peter. I could immediately sense the difference in his gaze: He saw no limits. He looked beyond what we were seeing that day. *Why couldn't I see the potential when it was clear to someone like Peter? What obstacle was in my mind keeping me from dreaming?* But by just being around someone like Peter, I could tell that my awareness was expanding. I was learning from someone who was free to dream and who acted on their dream.

A couple of weeks after returning to Denver from Vail, I was invited to a dinner party where I met Peter's wife, Betty Seibert. I'm not sure how it all happened, but because I had a teaching certificate, Betty offered me a job to be the headmaster of the as-yet-unconstructed Vail Country Day School. I was definitely meeting the right people in the right locations. It was as if spiritual advisors had led me to that point. There wasn't even a building yet, but I accepted the offer. I was fascinated with the idea of being a part of something new and growing.

It was an exciting time to be in Vail. Everything was moving fast. Cabins, restaurants, and new businesses were under rapid construction all around. Towers for a gondola on the top of the mountain that were supposed to be a two-year project were finished in a year. I eventually moved into a room in a new lodge with a food cafeteria. I didn't have to spend a dime from then on because food and lodging were provided.

Although I had no building to teach in and only about four students in the beginning, classes were held in any open space—bars, homes, or restaurants. We used the Calvert Education system, which was a project-based curriculum. New town developments and heavy snow were a constant detraction from our progress at school, but parents and students both were eager to make everything work. By the end of the second year, we had grown to twelve students, with a mix from the first to eighth grade. By that point, we had one classroom dedicated to our "school"—on the second floor of the fire department. We were ecstatic about the new environment. Having a desk, a chair for each student, and a blackboard in the front of the space felt like a luxurious setup compared with that of the past.

I loved teaching. Students loved my free style, and they responded well. We read books way beyond the students' level in other typical education systems, and we asked lots of open questions. Just as I was hungry to learn in my education, I wanted to teach them how to think independently as well.

I eventually moved up the ladder and became an assistant principal at Minturn High School. That was about the time I started to feel our education system had a serious flaw. The vision of my life of learning and expansion kept clashing with the things I was asked to do in that particular education system. After four years and one day, I realized that the position wasn't allowing me to grow. Most importantly, I wasn't making any money. I knew I was destined to be poor if I kept working in that position. *What is wrong with this picture?* I quit the job that day and never looked back.

I am happy that I witnessed part of the great history of an American town. It was an interesting turn of events happening in front of my eyes, and it had a great impact on how I directed my life. From a nonexistent village to a vibrant ski town, from poor to wealthy, from fixed to flexible mind, from regimentation to freedom, I knew that with this newer vision, I was ready for another big change in my life.

CHAPTER 7

Becoming a Businessman

I intuitively knew it was time to change the path of my life, even though I had no clue what that would be. A friend who owned three restaurants in Vail randomly suggested a commercial laundry. That sounded foreign yet enticing. The more I thought about this new business idea, the more it sounded like a great opportunity. With the town expanding with new hotels and restaurants, there was a greater need for a business to handle their laundry.

The asking price for starting a new commercial laundry in Eagle, Colorado, was $100,000—which I didn't have. The location was perfect, though, allowing the business to serve both Vail and Aspen. I borrowed $3,000 from my parents and $44,000 from the government. I was still about $55,000 short, but that didn't stop me from launching the new business. With the bank covering the rest of the loan, I became the CEO of my own business, Mountain Laundry Corporation.

The start of the business was rough as I didn't know anything about those commercial-size laundry machines. When I found a boiler in Denver to power and create steam for ironing the sheets, I immediately bought it. But it was monstrous in size, sitting on a cement slab. It had to be closer to the steam iron and moved inside a building before we could build the firebox. It was clear that it would have to be moved by a semitruck and unloaded by a crane. We used a railroad jack to lift and set the boiler on some steel pipes, but its weight crushed the pipes. A successful move was going to require steel rods cut by a blacksmith. I eventually I used my truck to push the boiler forward inch by inch.

Once we finally had it in place, I hired a stonemason to build the firebox, with only a picture on the cover of the container to guide me. It took persistence and tenacity, but finally, with only one glitch that required engineers from Denver to fix, I finally had steam to the iron.

The whole process took a year to complete.

In the meantime, I had to have three different hernia operations. As a veteran, I was treated in a military hospital, which was where I met nurse Patricia Gaudreault. She was an angel from heaven. We fell in love at first sight, got married, and moved to Vail. As such, she became the first nurse in Vail.

We acquired a five-acre plot in the middle of a large ranch, and it was there that Patricia and I started to build our house together, brick by brick. The site once had a water supply from a spring, but by that time, the spring was dry. We actually found a water source by using a forked branch as a water dowser. It felt like magic when the branch responded to the water source underneath the ground.

Over the next months, we made multiple trips to Denver with a semitruck to get supplies for the house building. When she wasn't working as a nurse, Patricia was a housebuilder six days a week. But we made sure to set aside one day for fishing or hiking. While I was doing yard work, she loved to read and paint images on a piece of old barn wood. We often sat on our foundation for our soon-to-be house and watched the sunset holding hands. Everything seemed right, and we were full of hope during those moments.

We ended up building a two-story house. In the fall, a herd of deer or elk gathered in front of the house. It was a magical place far and remote from city life. Patricia and I started to talk about starting a family. But life often throws a rock at you when you are least expecting it. In our bliss and happiness, we learned Patricia had cancer.

Losing Patricia wasn't how it was meant to be. It wasn't how I'd imagined telling the story of my fairy tale life. Except it was. I denied reality as long as I could. Even with numerous treatments, doctors' visits, and hospitals as our second residence, Patricia died soon after the discovery. I'd lost the love of my life just like that. No words can describe how I went through the valley of life without her and continued living without her. I was angry, depressed, anguished, lost, and terribly sad.

|||||||||||||||||||||||||||||||||||||||||||||||

I POURED EVERY OUNCE of my energy into the laundry business. I worked day and night, burying my sadness deep down. Between business trips and doing errands, I cried out loud in my car. But despite my loss, the business flourished. Soon, I had to buy more land to build a second building, which handled towels only. The ladies I hired were on top of what they were doing. Whenever I visited the site, there was a healthy sound of machines washing and drying and thousands of towels and sheets being folded daily. Employees ensured me that everything was under control. Fortunately, I never had to be there to manage every detail of the job.

My personal motto was, "Unless it is impossible, it is not worth my time and energy."

I allowed my employees to solve any challenge with whatever method they could come up with. I asked them to contact me if any task was beyond their comprehension. That way of managing a company made the workers feel a sense ownership of their work. It was their work, their team, and their methods. I was there only to encourage them to think for themselves.

At one point, I met a lawyer at a town meeting who spoke these words: "If what we do is against the law, I will change the law." At that very moment, I realized something within me had been unleashed, like an opening of a dam in a river. No more limitations held me back from dreaming and imagining what could be possible. My perspective on the world kept expanding.

I was living in an environment where seemingly impossible things happened every day. After ten years in Eagle, Colorado, I became one of the wealthiest men in the area, owning the largest commercial laundry business.

I know that one day, I will meet Patricia again. I will proudly tell her I made it through life okay and became a successful businessman. I will hold her tightly in my arms and tell her there wasn't a single second of my life that I didn't miss her.

Subconsciously, I have been waiting all my life to see her again and show her what I have done. She will be proud of her Allen, and I'm waiting to receive her warm gaze and that beautiful smile.

CHAPTER 8

The Inner Game of Life

It is interesting how a new chapter of one's life appears by itself if one listens to its small inner voice. Selling my commercial laundry business and moving to California came naturally to me. During this time, I got married to a wonderful woman, Margaret. We shared two passions: tennis and buying apartment buildings. Our future would include traveling back and forth between Colorado and California.

One of the guys I practiced tennis with had a real estate business and told me about the new listing of an apartment with sixteen units in Santa Ana. With prior experience managing apartments, it felt natural for me to buy apartments and have a rental business as the next chapter of my journey.

After our road trip, Margaret and I got to experience a vibrant new culture on the West Coast. We agreed that living closer to the ocean would provide us with a new quality of life. While we kept the rental business in Denver, we started a new residency near Newport Beach. We constantly hunted for a good deal on commercial buildings and apartments to buy and rent in the new area. Indeed, we started to learn how to play well with the market changes in the real estate industry and how to make the delicate move of borrowing money from the bank.

In any apartment or commercial building, we took great joy in improving on seemingly not-the-best-looking properties. Whether it was painting a few corners, fixing roofs, changing out cabinets, or changing the floors or lighting, we loved watching our buildings transform into a better version of themselves under our care. And Margaret, without any accounting background, was good at accounting: All her bookkeeping was on point to the penny. Women seem to know how to pay attention to the details much better than men. Surely and slowly, we built a solid foundation for wealth together as a team.

Also during this time, I became fascinated with tennis—not only the physical aspect of moving your body but also what you think as far as the opponents and yourself. It is ultimately a game of controlling your mind. Margaret and I bought rackets and started to practice in an empty court. The first ball I hit went over the net—and over the fence! Realizing my inept ability in this sport, my desire to learn and improve grew dramatically. I now had a new challenge: to become a decent tennis player.

We often played with other novice players casually, then started taking lessons with a pro. Whenever I felt the ball from a pro's serve, I realized the intensity and accuracy were on another level. As soon as we arrived in California, we joined the Palisades Tennis Club, where I biked and practiced tennis from sunrise to sunset 364 days a year.

I don't know where the intensity of the practice came from, but all I knew was that I wanted to improve myself—driven by curiosity, as I have always been. I loved the challenge and discovering what Allen was capable of. I thrived in the sensation of learning and the feel of my inner drive. If a farm boy from a rural town without running water could accomplish as much as I had done thus far, I knew there were many more layers in me that I could not fathom yet, but I knew they existed only if I didn't limit myself.

Taking lessons from Timothy Gallwey, the author of *The Inner Game of Tennis*, was an eye-opening experience. One of the most impactful things I learned from him was how you must understand the weakness and strength of your opponent and yourself. How you move your arms or feet must respond to data about your opponent that you study before and during the game. I always had an intensity about controlling my racket and ball and keeping an eye on the net in the middle. But the more I learned about tennis, the more importance I gave to questioning or understanding what my opponent thought or did. I needed to stay flexible to be able to change on the spot. The flexibility of thinking, as in my days at the University of Michigan, was one of the most valuable things I got from the "inner" game of tennis.

One summer, a European pro player arrived in Vail after competing in national tournaments. We decided to play a game together in a casual meeting at a court. He was a professional player who spent his year competing. I was an amateur player who had invested years of intense daily practice. During the match, I was in a flow state. He had "spent" his time in a court while I had "invested" my time in a court during the past year. I didn't assume I was a better player than he was, but in that very match, I was a better player mentally and physically. Perhaps there was a difference in spending versus investing time.

The most significant victory point for the match was my consistent push to his backhand, which I noticed as his weakness. I persistently served short or far outside the line, which made him move forward and to the outside. This was an unnatural movement for him, which resulted in a weak return. The more points I got, the more confused he became. This mental confusion attacked his confidence in the moment. My strategy for the match was to make him uncomfortable. What I beat him at was not the game of tennis but the game of the mind.

I realized being aware of one's mind is the key to winning a life match with oneself.

CHAPTER 9

Facing Resistance

A friend once mentioned that he had built a sailboat from a single sheet of plywood—including a sail, mast, and rudder. That weekend, he took me to sail in Cherry Creek Reservoir in Denver in his proud creation. When we reached the dock after the journey, he jumped out of the boat to tie it up. To my surprise, the boat suddenly blew away from the pier—with me sitting in it alone, confused, and moving quickly away. He frantically hollered at me what to do with a rudder. I didn't know what a rudder was, but I assumed that the lines attached to the sail could be a rudder. I grabbed them tightly. Instantly, I felt the wind and water resistance. I remember that was the first feeling of the resistance in the sailboat. Miraculously, I managed to get the boat back to the dock smoothly without any prior sailing knowledge.

My friend was impressed with what I had just done with this vessel. He kept talking about how naturally I handled the situation like an experienced sailor. And that was how I started sailing in my life.

Through decades of sailing all over the country and winning more than 20 sailing competitions with my beautiful balsa sailboat, I learned the lesson of a lifetime: the value of resistance. Just like we need to feel wind and water resistance to sail, we must confront resistance to grow in life. If we don't feel any resistance, we need to climb higher and push harder to feel it. On a peaceful day without wind, a sailboat cannot move. After all, resistance is a needed ingredient to move forward, a sign of growth.

I was always hunting for that feeling of resistance in life. Whenever I feel stuck, I look for the challenge to make me move forward. If life feels too easy, it is time for another challenge. Once you become a student of resistance, you will never stop growing into a better version of yourself. Any new inspiration meets resistance. Don't look for an easy route. Enjoy the wind on your face. I promise that you will get to some magical place beyond your imagination.

CHAPTER 10

Dance— The Secret to Life

Almost 40 years ago, Margaret and I were driving down a street in Costa Mesa, California, when we saw an advertisement for two lessons for the price of one in a local ballroom dance studio. *Ballroom dancing?* The concept sounded very out of my element, yet the deal seemed enticing and fun to try as a couple. We looked at each other and shouted with a smile, "Shall we dance?"

When we stepped into the studio for the first lesson, many professional and amateur dancers were taking lessons or practicing independently. From the looks on their faces, you could tell how much they dedicated themselves to improving and becoming better.

There was a mixture of seriousness and fun in the air. I was mesmerized by watching their movements, and at that moment, I felt something ignited within me instantly. Something about the whole scene of the dancing drew me to a new dimension in my life. I fell in love with ballroom dancing just like that.

Soon, I was introduced to three of the most outstanding teachers: Yuki, Kasia, and Rachel. Each had strengths in different dancing styles and offered me various aspects of dancing with their unique styles and personalities. From the waltz to the cha-cha and the rumba, the different types of dancing evoked different emotions and body expressions in me. Each was a distinct language of the movement. Even though Margaret and I started the trial lesson as a couple, it eventually became my sole journey with these three excellent teachers, and I ended up taking multiple weekly lessons.

I practiced my dance steps whenever I could: in my living room, on the street, or in the café waiting for my coffee. My head was filled with questions about being a better dancer or reviewing notes from previous lessons. Each lesson awakened me to think differently about my movement and how I felt about music or counting beats.

What I loved the most about dancing was that, ultimately, it wasn't about how accurately you perform your steps or learn your choreography; it was about how you let go and how gracefully you express yourself in music. There was an element of telling your story through movement. You speak the language of the body in music—primitively and instinctively.

Dancing fascinated me because your mind moves with music as your body moves. Your mind must be fluid to follow the music and express yourself as you desire. A stiff mind cannot accept an individual moment's constant changes or nuances between you and your partner. You must be ultimately connected with yourself yet able to disconnect from the outer world. Through the pursuit of improving myself in dance, I was able to tap into my soul, and I knew I was growing, expanding, and changing. When my body learned something new, my mind felt stretched. When I could understand a concept better in my mind, my body moved better to the rhythm of the music. In the end, I was learning how to dance through life.

At first, I started as a clumsy dancer who had no idea what I was doing. After four decades of practicing and learning from the best teachers, I won three number one Amateur Ballroom Dancer prizes and two second place prizes at many international ballroom competitions. I had to pinch myself whenever I looked at those trophies. Who is this guy who achieved these accomplishments in dance? How did I do that?

I believe there is a need to be free within all of us. Music helps to create and express the freedom to release and reveal our true feelings. Our bones and bodies wish to sing and dance. In my 90s, my days are still filled with dancing, taking lessons, practicing, and reviewing my notes. I feel that I am making progress all the time. Every day, I get to dance, make mistakes, and laugh.

The other day, someone in a café asked me about my secret to living a healthy life into my 90s. After learning about my age, he seemed amazed at my vitality. I smiled and whispered in his ear, "Go and dance. I promise: You will be happier."

Keep expanding your mind as wide as sky,

as deep as the sea.

CHAPTER 11

A Gift of Life

One day, one of my dance teachers recommended that I take a music lesson. She said it would improve my dancing. Music and dance are inseparable, but a talent for music was something I didn't think I had in me, nor was I really interested in it at that time.

So when I received a surprise birthday gift from my teacher in the form of a piano lesson from classical pianist Dr. Jeeyoon Kim, I honestly didn't know what to think or what I was expecting.

I was in my early 80s at that point, and I didn't expect I could learn something as complicated as playing piano, but I immensely enjoyed the conversation about music and life with Jeeyoon. And to my surprise, I found I could play a simple piano song after only a one-hour lesson! I also realized there was another world out there that I hadn't tapped into ever in my life: music. The rhythm, harmony, melody, and rich sound emanating from the piano rang deep within me as the lesson continued. It was like I was walking into a different dimension I had not yet discovered. I felt a primitive connection with my soul as if I had unconsciously known what to do. I was rejuvenated for weeks after that lesson. I was completely awakened by the sound of music.

Over the last decade, my friendship with Jeeyoon has grown into total admiration and respect for what she does—her music and her words. She has often told me that with enough repetition, something good will happen. I take her advice to heart as my daily mantra. If I feel stuck in something, I keep at it. I believe something magical will eventually happen as I release and allow myself to grow through the act of repetition. This mindset gives me confidence, and I know I am improving even when I can't see the progress that I am making.

I have a little digital keyboard in my house where I practice simple pieces daily, and I continue taking piano lessons from Jeeyoon. I enjoy making music on my own. I am getting better every day, even though I won't be a concert pianist—in this lifetime, anyway. Jeeyoon teaches lessons not only about music but also about life. Whenever I attend her piano concerts, re-read her book *Whenever You're Ready*, or listen to her public presentations, I am amazed at how she can create such an instant connection with a listener and draw people in with such a life force of energy. There is always a hint of softness in her delivery, which allows one's heart to accept her positivity more easily and with more conviction than if her approach were pedantic or pressured. I may be about five decades older than she is, but she illuminates a new path for me—a path that I keep moving forward on with unlimited possibilities.

About eight years ago, I had open-heart surgery to replace a heart valve. Even though it was an invasive surgery, my doctors said it needed to be done if I wanted to live longer. They agreed it was the right time to do it, when I had the ability to take on the physical challenge. I said yes and thought it would not be a big deal. I trusted in their opinions and advice.

For the next year and a half, I went through the most significant health challenge in my life. I didn't take the procedure as smoothly as doctors had anticipated. I fought back hard, but at the same time, I was losing the battle. I was getting tired of this mental and physical uphill. I was in and out of intensive care constantly. In the dark valley of losing consciousness, I heard my thoughts, deciding I would give up. *This will be my last breath. I've had a good life. It's time to go . . .* That was the moment I heard a small voice from the darkness. It was the voice of Jeeyoon. She was telling me, "I need you, Allen. Stay here, please. Don't go . . . "

I vividly remember recognizing that warm voice. It had an energy force to pull me into the other side of the world. Suddenly, I saw a light coming from the dark end of the tunnel I was in, giving me a lift to get up. I felt I could walk toward that—just a few more steps. I told myself, *I still have much to do in this life. Just follow that voice.*

I am forever indebted to Jeeyoon for bringing me back to this earth at that moment. Since then, my life has been a bonus, a gift I didn't think I had. I was reborn into a life that I get to live.

When I decided to embark on this book project a few years ago, I knew there wouldn't be a better person to help me tell the story of my life than Jeeyoon. Through this project, I felt I could relive my life through the stories I told. It was an exciting journey to learn more about myself than ever. Perhaps you might pick this book up and know that if Allen could do it, you can do whatever you wish to do in life. That has been my humble wish for the process of creating this book.

What I want to tell you is that life continues even when you are in your 90s. When people say ages are just numbers, trust me: That is true if you believe it. Our mind is the most giant hurdle we need to get over and develop. I feel the same when I look back on my teens, 20s, 30s, 50s, 80s—and even 90s. Every moment of my life has been worth having. Those experiences became a bridge to deepen my relationship with life and myself. Yes, I might not have as much energy as young people in their 20s, but I have a colorful, rich life. I am enjoying every second of what it offers.

When I look back on my life and even this morning, I notice there is one thing that drives my life. That is a sense of curiosity.

I am curious to learn more.
I am curious about how I can improve and become better.
I am curious about how I can help more people.
I am curious about experiencing this moment better.
I am curious about who I will be tomorrow.
I am curious about how you will transform yourself.
I am curious . . .

A Letter of Gratitude

Over the past year, I've had the privilege of being a part of Allen's memoir. When he first asked me to be a writer on this passion project, I was hesitant to accept the challenge. *Will I be able to express authentically what he went through? Can I be a good messenger for someone else's ideas and experiences?* Despite my doubts, in the end, I said yes. He convinced me that he was not looking for the best writer in the world to help deliver his story, but for his friend, Jeeyoon, to play that role. He trusted in my willingness to do my best and that my ability to connect with music would ultimately make me able to connect with his story.

Writing for someone else is very different from writing your own story. Instead of thinking about who *I* am, I needed to imagine my thoughts and emotions as if I were someone else. I would need to recreate scenes in my head from the mosaic of words that he provided me. Here was someone born in 1934 who went through the Great Depression, World War II, the Vietnam War, and the dramatic years of social justice changes. He lived to see incredible digital advances from the days when letters were the only form of communication to bulky computers and then to smartphones—computers in our pockets. I can't imagine what it must have been like growing up in a small town in Michigan where houses had no running water to becoming a person so full of rich life experiences who is still living a great healthy life at 91 years old in California.

I have had a wonderful time reliving his cherished memories. I kept wondering, *How many people can live to their 90s and still look back and remember while articulating their emotions and sharing wisdom from their life experiences?* The book's title, *Ever the Beginning*, is an expression of Allen's life motto. He lives each day he encounters as a beginning, a new adventure, and another personal transformation.

I still vividly remember the first day I met Allen. He came for a piano lesson wearing a cowboy hat and a warm yet mischievous smile. Though I was a teacher, I felt I was the one who gained life wisdom from him after just an hour of our piano lesson.

He asked, "What is your dream?"

I must admit that I was going through a deep and difficult valley of life at that time, and I honestly felt that dreaming about the future was a luxury I couldn't afford to even consider. Strangely enough, though, something in the delivery of his question made me realize that I needed to ask that core question to my soul once again. *What IS your dream, Jeeyoon?*

And with Allen's approach to my dream—which was *why NOT?*—I began to see that if you have a dream, it is your job to make it happen. Don't limit yourself. Just do it. Indeed, *why NOT?*

I responded to his energy, and I followed that light.

It was Allen's mindset of *why not?* that made it possible for me to perform at Carnegie Hall twice, make four solo piano albums, and publish three books in the United States and

Korea while performing actively around the globe. I established a global organization for piano teaching, Kim & Kim Piano Academy, where I reach thousands of students annually.

Allen has been a rock in my life. Whenever I feel that I can't do something, I hear his voice saying, "I trust you. I know you can change the world. Go and get 'em, girl. We all need a piece of Jeeyoon in this world. You are the heroine of your story."

No one in my life, including my parents, gave me this kind of unconditional love, support, and absolute trust in who I am, what I do, and what I can do. I can confidently say that Allen has saved my life and given me wings to fly over and beyond. I believe that one day, God decided to send me an angel in human form named Allen Brown.

A couple of weeks ago, I had a call from the ER that Allen had been admitted. He was in the intensive care unit, battling for his life with pneumonia and other complications. With each day that passed, considering his age, the doctors were not overly optimistic. I was devastated by the possibility of losing him. To other people, reaching your early 90s means a person has had a full, rich life if it is their time to go. However, I've realized that no matter what age Allen is, even if it's 120 years old, he will never have lived long enough for me to be ready to let him go.

Thankfully, as I write this note, Allen has made a good recovery. The doctors said it was like a miracle for him to come back around. This book project has been a personal journey for me as much as it must have been for Allen. I've gotten to know him much better than I did, and I feel that—with love and care—I gave him something back too. I had a short-term wish for this book: that Allen would be recovered fully by the time it was published. I got that wish and I got to see him smiling, reading, and holding his book in his hands. It was a blessing in my life that I will cherish forever.

I have another wish for this book: that whoever picks it up will get to experience Allen, gain wisdom from him, and remember Allen. He will live in everyone's hearts forever through his words and photographs. I often deeply feel the limitation of what we can express in words about what we truly feel inside. However, with my full heart, I want to say,

"Allen, thank you very much for being an important part of my life. You are the most generous, curious, gentle, funny, loving, and beautiful person I've ever met. You came into my life and let me fly over and beyond what I could ever dream. I promise you that I will continue living by your principles. I promise you that I will continue making music, teaching, and spreading your love through my own forms of art. I promise that you will always be in my soul and live forever within me and beyond this world. I love you!"

—Jeeyoon Kim

About Allen T. Brown

ALLEN T. BROWN was born in 1934 and has lived through many stages of life. At the age of 91, he shares his life's wisdom along with his black-and-white film photography in this book. He says, "I often shake my head at what has happened to me to allow me to live the life I am living now."

Allen never ceases growing and continues his education to this day, from becoming one of the top amateur ballroom dancers to learning classical piano. He maintains the courage to be curious and, of course, the courage to act on that curiosity. He feels that only the impossible is worthy of his time and mind.

Allen is the author of *Dancing Through Life.*

About Jeeyoon Kim

Jeeyoon Kim is a classical pianist, educator, author, and podcaster. She is passionate about creating classical music relevant to 21st-century audiences and becoming a bridge between music and her audience. She began studying the piano when she was just four years old, and her love of music propelled her through her undergraduate studies in piano performance in her native Korea. After moving to the United States, she received her master's of music and doctorate of musical arts in piano performance, with distinction, from Indiana University's renowned Jacobs School of Music.

Jeeyoon has shared her fresh perspective on classical piano performance with audiences at beloved venues such as Carnegie Hall in New York City, the Chamber Music Society in San Francisco, and the Stradivari Society in Chicago. She is the author of *Whenever You're Ready* and *Millions of Dreams* (백만 번의 상상). Her website is at www.jeeyoonkim.com.